USBORNE BIBLE TALES
NOAH'S ARK

Retold by Heather Amery

Illustrated by Norman Young
Designed by Maria Wheatley

Language consultant: Betty Root
Series editor: Jenny Tyler

This is Noah and his family.

Noah was a farmer who lived a long time ago. He had a wife and three sons. Each son had a wife.

Noah was a good man.

He worked hard, growing food for his family. Noah always did what God told him to do.

God talked to Noah.

He said, "The people are wicked. I'm going to flood the Earth and destroy them all, except you."

"Noah, you must build an ark."

"You must build it like this," said God. "Then you will save all the creatures in the world."

Noah started work.

His sons helped him. They marked out the shape of the ark on the ground and cut down trees.

Noah and his sons worked hard.

They made a wooden frame. They put tar
inside and outside the ark to make it waterproof.

At last, the ark was ready.

Noah and his sons loaded it with lots of food for their family and food for all the creatures.

Then the creatures came.

There were two of every kind. Noah stared at
them. "I didn't know there were so many," he said.

They all went into the ark.

"God was right," said Noah. "The ark He told me to build is just big enough for all of us."

Then it started to rain.

It rained for forty days and nights. The ark floated away with them all safely inside.

The flood lasted for months.

Noah said to a raven, "Go and find some dry land." The raven flew away but soon came back.

Later Noah sent off a dove.

It came back with a twig. Noah said, "The flood is over at last and everything is growing again."

Noah opened the door of the ark.

All his family and all the creatures rushed out. The sun was shining and the land was dry.

"Spread out and have families."

"Live all over the Earth," God said to the creatures.
"Noah, your family must do this too."

God put a rainbow in the sky.

"That's my sign," said God. I promise I'll never flood the whole Earth again." "Thank you," said Noah.

This edition first published in 2003 by Usborne Publishing Ltd, 83-85 Saffron Hill, London EC1N 8RT, England. www.usborne.com
Copyright © 2003, 1996 Usborne Publishing Ltd.